OFFICIALLY
WITHDRAWN

TOOLS FOR CAREGIVERS

- **ATOS:** 0.6
- **GRL:** C
- **WORD COUNT:** 44

- **CURRICULUM CONNECTIONS:** animals, habitats

Skills to Teach

- **HIGH-FREQUENCY WORDS:** a, has, is, it, long, mom, this
- **CONTENT WORDS:** baby, calf, eats, follows, giraffe, grows, learns, leaves, legs, neck, reaches, runs, spots, tall(er), tongue, trees
- **PUNCTUATION:** exclamation points, periods
- **WORD STUDY:** long /e/, spelled ea (eats, leaves, reaches); long /e/, spelled ee (trees); long /o/, spelled ow (follows); multisyllable words (baby, giraffe, taller); r-controlled vowels (learns)
- **TEXT TYPE:** information report

Before Reading Activities

- Read the title and give a simple statement of the main idea.
- Have students "walk" though the book and talk about what they see in the pictures.
- Introduce new vocabulary by having students predict the first letter and locate the word in the text.
- Discuss any unfamiliar concepts that are in the text.

After Reading Activities

Ask the readers to think about the environment that is the focus of the book. Do they know what Africa is like? Invite them to discuss what makes a safari and then to name other animals and plants they think might live in Africa. How do giraffes survive in Africa?

Tadpole Books are published by Jump!, 5357 Penn Avenue South, Minneapolis, MN 55419, www.jumplibrary.com

Copyright ©2019 Jump. International copyright reserved in all countries. No part of this book may be reproduced in any form without written permission from the publisher.

Editor: Jenna Trnka **Designer:** Anna Peterson

Photo Credits: Imphilip/Dreamstime, cover; Jen Watson/Shutterstock, 1; Simon Fletcher/Dreamstime, 2–3, 16tl; kotomiti/CanStock, 4–5, 16bm; Nick Fox/Shutterstock, 6–7; Mees Kuiper/Shutterstock, 8–9, 16tr; Bob Suir/Dreamstime, 10–11, 16bl; 3plusX/Shutterstock, 12–13, 16br; Minden Pictures/SuperStock, 14–15; Nik Merkulov/Shutterstock, 16tm.

Library of Congress Cataloging-in-Publication Data
Names: Nilsen, Genevieve, author.
Title: Giraffe calves / by Genevieve Nilsen.
Description: Tadpole edition. | Minneapolis, MN: Jump!, Inc., (2019) | Series: Safari babies | Includes index.
Identifiers: LCCN 2018024753 (print) | LCCN 2018027522 (ebook) | ISBN 9781641282390 (ebook) | ISBN 9781641282376 (hardcover : alk. paper) | ISBN 9781641282383 (paperback)
Subjects: LCSH: Giraffe—Infancy—Juvenile literature.
Classification: LCC QL737.U56 (ebook) | LCC QL737.U56 N55 2019 (print) | DDC 599.63813/92—dc23
LC record available at https://lccn.loc.gov/2018024753

GIRAFFE CALVES

by Genevieve Nilsen

TABLE OF CONTENTS

tadpole books

GIRAFFE CALVES

This baby is tall.

calf

It is a giraffe calf!

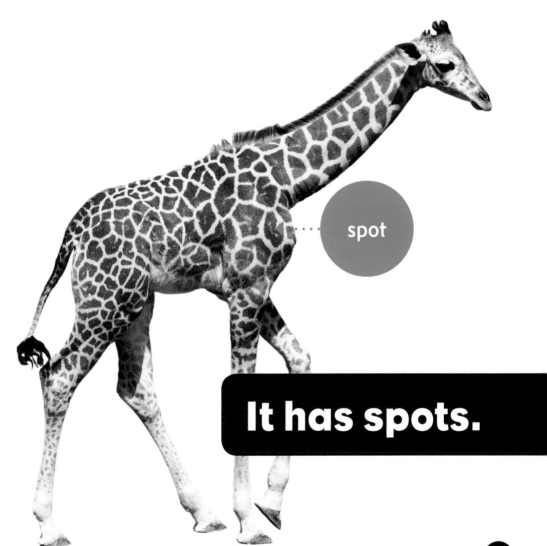

spot

It has spots.

It follows mom.

mom

It learns.

It has long legs.

It runs.

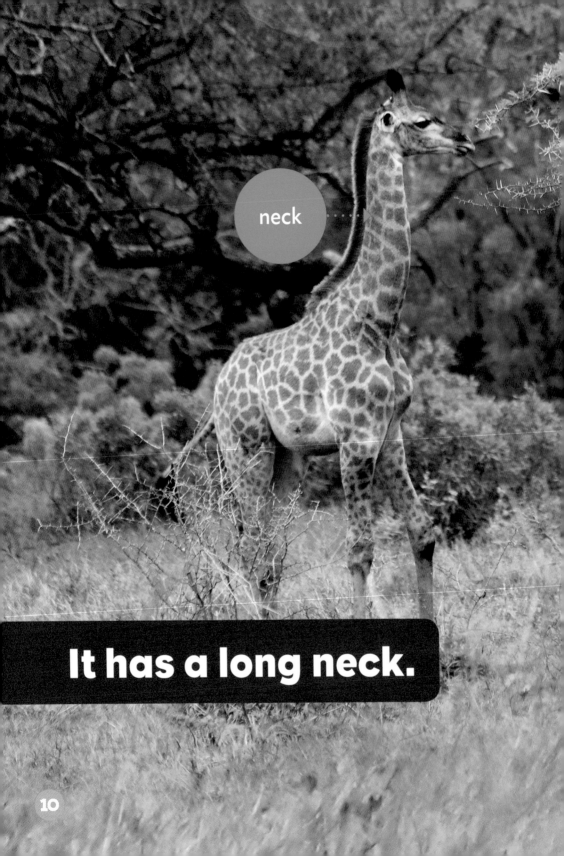

neck

It has a long neck.

It reaches trees.

It has a long tongue.

It eats leaves.

It grows taller!

WORDS TO KNOW

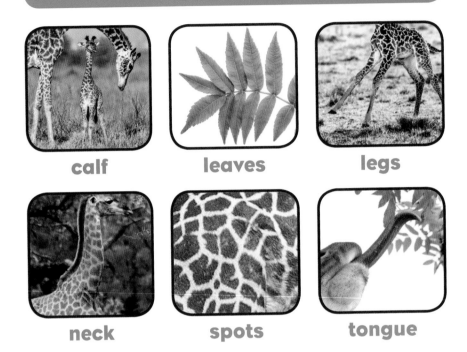

calf

leaves

legs

neck

spots

tongue

INDEX